DAILY MANTRAS

THE
DREAM
LIFE
PROJECT

Copyright © 2024 Cecilia Huang
First published 2024
The Dream Life Project
https://thedreamlifeproject.co
ISBN: 978-1-7638175-1-7

All rights reserved. No parts of the publication may be reproduced, distributed, or transmitted in any form or by any means including photocopying, recording, or other electronic or mechanical methods without prior written permission from the publisher.

Design and layout by Cecilia Huang

101 little ways to spark joy

DAILY MANTRAS

CECILIA HUANG

introduction

In the quiet corners of your life, amidst the rush and clamor of everyday existence, lies a treasure that is both pure and innate: joy. It's a gentle whisper that beckons you to pause, to breathe deeply, and to embrace the beauty of the present moment. This book is a celebration of this elusive, yet profoundly accessible essence.

Joy is not confined to grand gestures or rare occasions; it can manifest in the smallest of moments, through the gentle act of presence, the patience of waiting, the appreciation of the minutiae, and the warmth of genuine connections. It is in the shared laughter with a friend, the comfort of a pet's affection, the serenity of a sunset, and the quiet solace of our inner world.

This book invites you to explore how joy can emerge from the mundane and the extraordinary alike. It encourages you to find delight in the daily mantras that nurture hope, optimism, and a deep reverence for the wonder of life.

By committing to practices of gratitude, generosity, movement, and beauty, you'll uncover how these seemingly simple acts can weave joy into the fabric of your everyday experience.

As you turn these pages, may you discover new ways to invite joy into your life, finding it in the spaces between, in the moments of stillness, and in the vibrant tapestry of connection. Each little way is a step towards creating a dream life - a life filled with the radiant glow of joy.

Welcome to a journey of daily mantras, where joy is not just a fleeting visitor but a cherished companion, guiding you towards a fulfilled and beautiful life.

Cecilia

Joy is what happens to us when we allow ourselves to recognise how good things really are.

MARIANNE WILLIAMSON

1

let joy be

Be courageous and stay curious in times of loss, strife or sorrow. Amid discomfort or tragedy, there are opportunities for deep connection, reflection, regeneration and even laughter.

2

see the good

It's not always easy to see the positive in life, but when you make a conscious effort to acknowledge the goodness, joy is often found in the present moment, in even the smallest things.

3

keep your cool

Beat the heat with sweet cool treats. Anytime is always a good time for ice cream, whether it's a hot summer day or a moment of indulgence; for young, old and even your four-legged friends; the joy of ice cream knows no bounds.

4

let joy work

It is in the effort, the struggle, and the perseverance that you find happiness. While the ultimate victory brings temporary satisfaction, it is the process of overcoming challenges that bring lasting joy. Find joy in the journey, not just in the destination.

5

step out of comfort zone

Comfort zones are not about comfort, they are about fear. Break the chains of fear to get outside. Once you do, you will learn to enjoy the process of taking risks and growing in the process. Dare to begin today.

6

take a risk

While staying safe on the ground may feel comfortable, it can also be limiting and dull. By daring to climb higher, you can experience new perspectives and opportunities, and reach your full potential. You can't fall if you don't climb. But there's no joy in living your whole life on the ground.

7

be flexible

Flexibility is often more effective than rigidity in overcoming challenges. Embracing resilience through adaptation allows you to endure and thrive in the face of adversity, much like the willow that bends but does not break.

8

see the silver linings

With each setback, take a moment to reflect on the many blessings in your life. Practising gratitude is a powerful antidote to despair. It reminds you that even in difficult times, there are always silver linings, a ray of sunshine amidst the storm, a glimmer of hope amidst the darkness.

When some things go wrong, take a moment to be thankful for the many things that are going right.

ANNIE GOTTLIEB

9

celebrate small wins

No matter how small the triumph, give yourself a little tap on your back. Your future self will thank you for banking the feel-good moment. You'll be able to tap into your positive memory reserves when times get tough.

10

write down joyful moments

Capture the funny-sweet things kids say, loved-up things our partner says, a resonant quote or affirmation, or a line from a poem. When you reflect on them you'll ping a string of joy.

11

throw a party

'Just because' is perhaps one of the best reasons to shindig! Celebrate: the first day of spring, your grandma's birthday, your best friend's new job, someone arriving or departing, hooking a new lover or releasing an old one.

12

walk in nature

Walk gently among the sounds of nature and let it soothe your busy brain. If you ever feel a little overwhelmed, take a stroll as it will lift your mood. The company of flora and fauna aid dreamy imaginings to drop in.

13

go barefoot

Kick off your shoes and dig your toes into the earth. Reconnect yourself with nature, it helps you stabilise the electricity in your body, lower blood pressure and boost immunity. Feel grounded, release stress and invite joy.

14

dance

Dance is your pulse, your heartbeat, your breathing. It's the rhythm of your life. It connects you with your body, with others and with the world. Dance allows your body to move freely, express your emotions, celebrate your victories and release your sorrows.

15

see a sunrise

Watching the dawn break is awe-inspiring. No matter how many times you've seen it before, watching the sun rise is a sure-fire way to greet the day with joy. May your smile rise with the sun and illuminate your day.

16

look and listen closely

Look closely at how a caterpillar chomps, or a dragonfly hovers. Eavesdrop on backyard birds or listen intently to the sounds of summer. Get up close and pay attention to the many faces of nature, you may even discover new friends.

17

free up space

Release people, projects, jobs and belongings to free up space in your world. Allow new opportunities to land and enable you to make choices better suited to your time, purpose, values and beliefs.

18

smile

Sometimes, your joy lights up your face like a beacon, spreading good vibes wherever you go. But other times, even if you're feeling a bit down, just putting on a smile can kickstart a chain reaction of happiness, turning your day around.

19

spend with care

Remove expenses that do not impact your quality of life. Cancel unused subscriptions; trade books with friends to reduce the cost per read; complement your wardrobe staples with some op shop bargains.

20

be a change agent

Never was there a more important time to put the planet first. Make moves towards a more sustainable future by choosing responsible companies, you become an advocate of a fair and just world for all.

21

start a side hustle

Add a side stream to pay for your adventures or fast-track your financial independence. Review your passions and skills to identify where you could be adding greater value to your bank account balance. It also allows you to explore new interests and talents.

22

keep a light heart

Just like any journey, life is not without its bumps and detours. Enjoy the ride and do not take things too seriously. Live fully with a sense of humour and playfulness will make your journey more enjoyable. Find laughter in everyday moments. Choose to see the lighter side of life.

23

be like a child

Smile with your heart, remove your shoes, dance in the rain, colour in, play a board game, picnic at home, make a cubby and read your book in it, observe the smallest creatures, take a bubble bath, eat cake, daydream...

24

fall in love

The excitement of falling in love, the contentment of being in love, and even the pain of falling out of love are all unique and enriching experiences. Even the least desirable part of love is far better than never having experienced it at all. Let yourself fall in love all over again.

25

wake up to a fresh perspective

As you awaken, allow yourself to be enveloped by the beauty of the morning sun and your surroundings. This fresh perspective infuses your life with delight, setting a positive tone for the hours ahead.

26

be vulnerable

Joy sits in the wings of freedom when you honestly admit and acknowledge your thoughts and feelings. Be willing to see and share your hurt, embarrassment, fears, loves, passions and desires.

27

add love

Honesty fosters trust and clarity, while love provides compassion and understanding. Together, they create a powerful force that can resolve conflicts, strengthen relationships, and bring peace to difficult circumstances.

28

celebrate birthdays

Age is just a number, and the true measure of your life is the quality of your experiences. Spending time with your loved ones, enjoying shared experiences and making new memories together is much more fulfilling than simply adding another year to your age.

29

welcome surprises

Each day brings its surprises, whether in the form of joy or sorrow. Welcome the unexpected moments, open new places in your hearts, and connect more deeply with others. Embrace life's surprises, welcome new friends and celebrate shared humanity.

30

see the joy in sorrow

Even amid pain, loss, and grief, moments of joy can be found. The strange polarity of sorrow is that it often coexists with gratitude. Your grief is a reflection of the one you loved. Acknowledging this duality allows you to create a space for healing.

31

savour what you have

Take a step back and appreciate the things that bring you joy, whether it's a beautiful garden, a loved one, or simply a quiet moment of solitude. You never know when you might lose what you have, so cherish it while you can.

32

share stories

Amass memories of life's funny and pivotal moments, then share these stories. Through storytelling, you create bonds with others, celebrate your journeys, and pass down wisdom that can inspire future generations.

33

be inspired by yourself

When you find inspiration within yourself, life becomes easier. Treat yourself with kindness, understanding, and support, and fuel your inner drive with greater ease and confidence.

34

create beauty

Infusing colour, quality, and sensory delights into everyday moments. Create a rainbow of colours with a fruit or crudité platter, wear bright patterns, use quality tools, share a slow kiss, and ensure pleasant scents in your environment.

35

forget the big picture

Optimists find joy in the most ordinary moments. Appreciate the simple things, like a warm cup of tea or a beautiful sunset; value a collection of small pleasures over the pursuit of one grand happiness.

36

be silly

Playtime isn't just for kids. Do yourself a favour, step out of your grown-up bubble and play. It's a great way to de-stress, stimulate the brain and keep you feeling vibrant, fostering trust, safety and intimacy in your relationships.

37

back yourself

Believe in yourself to unlock your potential for curiosity, wonder, and spontaneous delight. Trust in your worth, take risks and embrace new experiences with confidence. Be open to a life that inspires and uplifts you.

38

be humble

Keep perspective, listen, go last, apologise, praise others and ask for advice. Humility opens the door to new opportunities. Extend admiration for someone or something. It feels wonderfully good to do and terrific to receive.

39

empower others

Let others see their greatness through your eyes, empower them to see the potentials in themselves. Reflect admiration and foster positive, supportive relationships that highlight the best qualities in everyone.

40

streamline everyday tasks

Life hacks lighten stress levels and ease your load, so you have more time to do what you love. Whether it's for organising your time, home or to-do list, or engaging your brain with creative ideas.

41

choose your crew

Find individuals who push you to be better, challenge your thinking, and inspire you to grow. When you spend time with those who bring out the best in you, you can achieve greater things than you ever imagined.

42

do a daily practice

Your daily practice helps you to be attuned to the day and revel in life. Yoga, writing a journal, meditation, stretching, breathwork, tai chi, year-round swimming, surfing, reading or walking, will lift you up when things feel less joyful.

43

make food fun

Lighten up, cut loose, and be a little silly. Add a fruit face to your breakfast bowl, spell something with your peas, make a cat-shaped pancake or write yourself a lunch box love note.

44

breathe to bliss

Breathing can stimulate and also calm the nervous system. Start by simply drawing your awareness to your breath and slowing your breath down. Breathe in to the count of four and then out similarly for 10 cycles.

45

rest

Rest is good for your heart and brain, and it could even add days to your life. Complement a good sleep with rest during the day. Take time to stare into space, move slowly and gently, decompress and breathe with awareness.

46

be a sniffer dog

Joy often hides in the small, everyday moments, waiting to be discovered. Whether it's the scent of fresh flowers, the laughter of a loved one, or a beautiful sunset, keeping your senses tuned to joy enhances your appreciation of life.

47

read books

Reading for pleasure is pure joy. Allow yourself to be transported by characters, communities, adventures and worlds. Lose yourself to a book as fictional or real-life experiences allow you to walk the lives of others.

48

make something

Take joy in the process of making. Make a new garden, write a letter, paint a picture, put up a tent, whittle some wood, experiment with a new recipe. Lose yourself in flow, express your true nature freely.

49

revel in creativity

When you create, you tap into a wellspring of creativity and imagination that lies within you. It is not about the money, fame, or recognition, but about the sheer pleasure of making something and sharing it with the world.

50

trust in life

The world is complex, but also full of wonders. You can choose how you perceive the world. When you approach it with faith, trust, and a sense of childlike wonder, you may find that life becomes more beautiful.

51

keep trying

It is never too late to pursue your passions and to actualise your true potential. Every day is a fresh start. Each moment offers a fresh opportunity to embrace your dreams and step into the life you have envisioned for yourself.

52

create a personal board

Choose a handful of people to sit on your 'personal board'. They are people whom you trust, who are able to offer varied perspectives, have the time to listen to you, and are willing to be honest. They also double your happiness when you win.

53

listen deeply

Full-body listening fosters genuinely deeper and more trusted relationships. Park your own agenda, and with no immediate need to communicate your thoughts, observe how you begin experiencing relationship breakthroughs.

54

share meals

Food, family and friends – it's what memories and mirth are made of. Sit together with your household for at least one meal a day. The dining table provides an opportunity for connection. Check in and share the day's objectives, achievements and insights.

55

eat with thanks

Your digestive system will thank you when you acknowledge where your meal came from, who made it and the company you keep when you eat. Spare a thought of thanks when slicing your salad or chopping juicy fruit and produce.

56

spend time together

Joy is not something that can be fully appreciated alone. It multiplies when you spend quality time together. Sharing joy brings your family and friends closer together and helps you form deeper connections with them.

57

belly laugh

Just as a flash of lightning can break through a dark and gloomy sky, bringing a moment of brightness and hope, so too can mirth bring a spark of joy. The moment of laughter can lift your spirits and help you see the world in a positive light.

58

love yourself

Loving yourself can be one of the hardest, yet most important things you'll ever do. Value and care for your own needs, wants and desires. It isn't about being selfish. It's about making sure you have time to recharge and to have the energy and resources to be there for others.

59

take five minutes in nature

When life gets overwhelming, sometimes the best thing you can do is step outside and take a breather. Hit the reset button for your mind. Nature has an amazing way of soothing your soul and putting things back into perspective. Make sure you prioritise time outdoors to recharge and refresh, even when life gets hectic.

Step outside for a while — calm your mind. It is better to hug a tree than to bang your head against a wall continually.

RASHEED OGUNLARU

60

give time

Dedicate time to your friends, family, cause or community group. Encourage and inspire others to be braver, stronger, kinder, and smarter. There's immense joy in the company of someone willing to give their undivided attention.

61

make new friends

Cultivate new friends by following up with someone you met but got busy and never managed to reconnect with. Pick up where you left off. New friendships bring about new ideas, thoughts and knowledge.

62

give compliments

A spontaneous and authentic compliment can bestow the gift of happiness on someone's day. The best part is that compliments are free, yet their impact is priceless. Being sincere in your delivery will ensure your compliment has genuine resonance.

63

seek out love

When you experience love, you feel a deep sense of fulfilment, and you want to celebrate that feeling with those you care about most. Whether it's a romantic relationship, a close friendship, or a bond between family members, love can make a great celebration out of your life.

do a little dance

When things get tough and the sweetness seems to fade away, that's when you need to shake things up a bit. Stick a sticker on your nose and bust out a funky dance. Inject some fun and silliness into your days, even when life feels a bit sour.

Life is sweet when you pay attention. When it doesn't seem sweet, put a sticker on your nose and do a funky dance.

WHITNEY SCOTT

65

find meaning

Everyone has unique talents and passions that, when discovered, can bring immense joy. The journey of life is to discover your gifts and use them to make a positive impact on the world. The joy of life comes from sharing your gifts with others and making a difference in their lives.

66

give what you wish for

Be willing to extend to others what you want to experience. If you crave kindness, be kind. If you need more love in your life, deliver love in lorry loads. If you wish you were more respected, be more respectful.

67

learn from everything

Life's like a lemon tree sometimes, it throws a few sour fruits your way, but hey, free lemons! It's about seeing the bright side, making lemonade out of lemons, or maybe just enjoying the zest. Those lemons might just add a little flavour to your day.

68

enjoy me time

'Me time' can be hard to come by. Taking a luxurious, lingering bath is a way to say 'thank you' to your body for all the hard work it puts in for you, every day. Light candles, diffuse essential oils and don't skimp on the bubble bath. Allow all your senses to soak up the moment.

69

take a stroll

Put on your walking shoes and leave your headphones at home. Tune in to your body, become aware of your gait as you walk, and pay attention to what is around you. Look for beauty, and appreciate it. When your mind wanders off, come back to the rhythm of your stride and the sensation of your soles hitting the ground.

Where you put your attention is where you put your life.

SCOTT BARRY KAUFMAN

70

look up

Gaze at the stars, feel your connection with the universe, and remind yourself of the miracle of your existence. Get out into the forest, look up at tall trees, waterfalls, and lush hills. When you focus on the beauty of nature, the mind quietens, making it harder to get tangled up in your thoughts.

71

watch the sunset

As the sun dips down into the horizon soaking the surrounding sky in ice-cream colours, you are afforded a wonderful opportunity for a mindful reminder that every day offers you a new end and a new beginning. All you need to do is to step outside and look up at the sky.

look at a flower

Beauty isn't just something you see with your eyes, it's like a balm for the soul, soothing and uplifting. When you take the time to appreciate the beauty around you, whether it's in nature, art, or the kindness of others, you're hitting the reset button for your mind.

73

open your arms

Consider every person who crosses your path as a guide, a messenger from beyond. They arrive not by chance, but by design, each carrying a lesson, a blessing, or a reminder. Whether they stay for a moment or a lifetime, their presence shapes your journey and expands your understanding of the world.

74

make grateful moments

Instead of instantly scrolling on the phone when waiting in line, try to set your phone aside, take a deep breath and start listing in mind the things that you're grateful for or that are especially bringing you joy that day.

Be thankful for what you have;
you'll end up having more.
If you concentrate on what you
don't have, you will never, ever
have enough.

OPRAH WINFREY

75

embrace the power of 'yes'

When you hold onto a belief that things will work out, your vision becomes attuned to opportunities that align with that belief. Conversely, if you anticipate failure, obstacles seem to manifest at every turn. Your mind has the power to influence the outcome. Say 'yes' even in the face of uncertainty.

76

choose the way you see things

Life often comes with circumstances beyond your control, situations that demand acceptance and adaptation. In those moments, you're faced with a choice: to resist or to evolve. While you may not have control over external events, you always retain the power to shape your internal landscape.

77

start your day in gratitude

Starting the day with gratitude can set the tone for everything that follows. By making it a habit to note and write down three things you're thankful for each morning, you create space for positivity, no matter how the day unfolds. Do this daily and observe the positive impacts.

78

take a lunch break

Don't be tempted to push through. Taking even a 15-minute break will pay dividends later in the day. When you take a walk or relax during the day, you are better able to concentrate while at work. It will also decrease your stress and tiredness at the end of your day.

79

count each day as a life

It's easy to forget that time is limited, but when you let that sink in, it's a wake-up call to start living life to the fullest. It's about squeezing every drop of joy, love, and adventure out of each day. You never know when your time will be up. Cherish every moment as if it were your last.

80

clear your desk

A clutter-free desk mirrors inner calm. The more clutter on display, the more easily you'll be distracted. Make it easy on yourself and discard the muddle and clutter. It's a simple act that invites focus and reduces the mental load.

81

declutter one area

Go through one area of your home and make three piles. One pile is to give away to friends and family. One pile is to donate to charity. One pile is to keep. Everything in this pile should have a defined place and purpose in your home.

82

put down your phone

When you find yourself reaching for your phone, stop for a moment and check in with yourself about your purpose. If there is no reason, or it's not a compelling one, then put the phone down and make better use of your time.

83

take a problem on a walk

When your thoughts are tangled, stepping away can provide clarity. Take your problem on a walk with you. Moving your body will complement your mental efforts and the change in perspective may trigger your subconscious to deliver a solution.

84

breathe deeply

Take a deep breath and pause to notice the beauty in the air, the mountains, the trees, and the people. It's in those moments of presence, where you connect fully with the world, that you realise happiness isn't a destination, but a feeling you can access anytime you choose to truly see and feel.

85

feast with focus

Before you start to eat, take a moment to be mindful of all the chains of agriculture, transport, storage and distribution that contribute to bringing the food onto your plate. Appreciate not only all the people involved but how the food will bring nutrition and strength into your body.

86

devise a bedtime routine

For a peaceful and nourishing sleep, devise a bedtime routine beginning one hour before bedtime. Including dimming the lights, shutting off any screens, reading a chapter of a book or listening to relaxing jazz, putting on your softest clothes and snuggling up.

87

be a parachute

Your mind is like a parachute, just waiting to catch the wind and take you on a wild ride. But it can only do its job when it's open and ready to soar. Open up your mind to new possibilities, let it embrace curiosity, learning, and growth, and spread its wings and fly.

Minds are like parachutes. They only function when they open.

THOMAS DEWAR

88

choose love over fear

Instead of fearing the inevitable, use that time to shower your families with love, treasure your friendships, and truly live your life to the fullest. These moments are what truly matter in the grand tapestry of life.

> We spend precious hours fearing the inevitable. It would be wise to use that time adoring our families, cherishing our friends and living our lives.
>
> MAYA ANGELOU

89

show appreciation

Appreciation isn't just about saying "thank you" or giving a pat on the back, it's a magical mirror that reflects the excellence in others right back at you. When you appreciate someone's talents or qualities, you're also claiming a piece of that excellence for yourself, making it part of who you truly are.

90

cultivate the notion of 'enough'

Learn to recognise your desires and observe them. Try to resist the need for more or ownership of objects that you desire but don't truly need. Cultivate the idea that you have enough by creating a mantra 'I have everything I need' which you can use in moments of temptation.

91

just listen

Listening is a simple, free gift to give, but is an invaluable one to receive. In a world where everyone seems eager to speak, being the person who listens can provide relief and connection. Sometimes, all a person needs is a listening ear, someone to be there while they unburden themselves.

92

choose to be kind

Sometimes, you may find yourself at a crossroads where you must decide between proving your point or extending kindness. Choosing kindness over being right can soften hearts. Choose compassion and understanding, even when faced with the temptation to assert your correctness.

93

be honest

While honesty may not always be easy or popular, it ensures that the connections you form are genuine. When you pair it with respect and consistent actions, you draw the right people into your life. True friends value and reciprocate honesty, creating bonds that stand the test of time.

Being honest might not get you a lot of friends but it will always get you the right ones.

JOHN LENNON

94

soak up the small things

The laughter shared with loved ones, the warmth of a cup of tea, and the beauty of a sunset, are the little things that weave together the fabric of your life. Cherish and find joy in these small moments, and savour the small wonders that bring richness and depth to your life.

95

accept kindness

Kindness often leads to more kindness. When you accept a kind gesture from someone else you are, in turn, doing a kindness. When someone holds the door open for you, they experience a warm feeling from doing a nice thing. Enjoy the gift that they have given you. Then passing the goodwill on.

96

share your gifts

In the search for meaning in life, you discover your unique gifts and talents. The true purpose of life lies not merely in the discovery of this gift, but in the act of sharing it with others. By using your gifts to uplift and inspire others, you find fulfilment for yourself.

The meaning of life is to find your gift. The purpose of life is to give it away.

PABLO PICASSO

97

love yourself unapologetically

Love yourself unapologetically and do things that add quality and beauty to life. A healthy self-love means you have no compulsion to justify to yourself or others why you take vacations, why you sleep late, why you buy new shoes, and why you spoil yourself from time to time.

98

value your self-talk

What you whisper to yourself in the quiet moments is a real game-changer. Those inner whispers pack a serious punch. They've got this sneaky way of shaping your world way more than what you broadcast to the crowd. Keeping your self-talks positive and powerful.

99

age gracefully

There is beauty in growing older, a kind of peaceful acceptance that comes with time. Wrinkles, like the lines in a well-loved book, tell stories of joy, struggle, and wisdom. The radiant glow of a happy, seasoned soul is an extraordinary thing to witness.

100

enjoy the elements

Each type of weather brings its unique energy, and every moment holds something to be appreciated. Sunshine lifts your spirit, rain nourishes the earth, wind awakens your senses, and snow invites you to slow down and reflect. Learn to embrace the beauty of each condition, finding joy in the surprises nature offers.

101

embrace the season

Immerse yourself in the present moment, savour the air you breathe, the flavours you taste, and the beauty of the natural world. Allow yourself to be influenced by the earth's beauty and wisdom, and align yourself with the rhythm of life.

Live in each season as it passes; breathe the air, drink the drink, taste the fruit, and resign yourself to the influence of the earth.

HENRY DAVID THOREAU

from Cecilia

Through daily rituals, words of empowerment, and affirming quotes, I hope to support and inspire you to live your dream life filled with moments of reflection, self-discovery, and love.

If you found this book helpful, please review and share it. That helps it find its way to those who need it. This would mean a lot to me. Thank you.

Connect with me:
https://thedreamlifeproject.co
@dreamlifeproject_

www.ingramcontent.com/pod-product-compliance
Lightning Source LLC
Chambersburg PA
CBHW061750070526
44585CB00025B/2847